I LOVE OUR LAND

Carol Greene

Enslow Elementary, an imprint of Enslow Publishers, Inc.
Enslow Elementary® is a registered trademark of Enslow Publishers, Inc.

Copyright © 2013 by Enslow Publishrs, Inc.

All rights reserved.

No part of this book may be reproduced by any means without the written permission of the publisher.
Original edition published as *Caring for Our Land* in 1991.

Library of Congress Cataloging-in-Publication Data

Greene, Carol.
  I love our land / by Carol Greene.
     p. cm. — (I love our Earth)
  Summary: "Find out why our land is important, and how people can protect it"—Provided by publisher.
  Includes index.
  ISBN 978-0-7660-4040-3
  1. Landscape protection—Juvenile literature. 2. Land use—Environmental aspects—Juvenile literature. 3. Environmental protection—Juvenile literature. 4. Environmental protection—Citizen participation—Juvenile literature. I. Title.
  QH75.G715 2012
  333.73'13—dc23
                    2011023713

Future editions:
Paperback ISBN 978-1-4644-0137-4
ePUB ISBN 978-1-4645-1044-1
PDF ISBN 978-1-4646-1044-8

Printed in the United States of America
042012 Lake Book Manufacturing, Inc., Melrose Park, IL
10 9 8 7 6 5 4 3 2 1

To Our Readers: We have done our best to make sure all Internet Addresses in this book were active and appropriate when we went to press. However, the author and the publisher have no control over and assume no liability for the material available on those Internet sites or on other Web sites they may link to. Any comments or suggestions can be sent by e-mail to comments@enslow.com or to the address on the back cover.

Enslow Publishers, Inc., is committed to printing our books on recycled paper. The paper in every book contains 10% to 30% post-consumer waste (PCW). The cover board on the outside of each book contains 100% PCW. Our goal is to do our part to help young people and the environment too!

Photo Credits: iStockphoto.com: © Carmen Martínez Banús, p. 16, © Jani Bryson, p. 19; Shutterstock.com, pp. 1, 3, 4–5, 7, 8, 10–11, 13, 14–15, 20, 21.

Cover Photo: Shutterstock.com

Enslow Elementary
an imprint of
Enslow Publishers, Inc.

40 Industrial Road
Box 398
Berkeley Heights, NJ 07922
USA

http://www.enslow.com

Contents

What Is It? 5

Why Is Land Important? 6

What Can Happen to Land? 10

What Can We Do? 17

What Can You Do? 20

Words to Know 22

Learn More:
  Books and Web Sites 23

Index 24

Soil covers much of our land.

What Is It?

We need it for food. We need it for a home. We need it because it is beautiful. What is it? **Land**.

More than half the earth is covered with water. What isn't covered with water is land. Some of this land is just rocks. Some is just sand. But much of the earth's land is covered with soil.

Soil is made of different kinds of ground-up rock, dead plants and animals, air, and water. All land is important. But land covered with soil is most important to the living things on earth.

Why Is Land Important?

People, plants, and animals need a place to live. Seaweed, sharks, and shrimp make their homes in water. But roses, bears, and people must live on land.

People and animals also get much of their food from the land. Corn, apples, and peanuts all grow on the land. Cows eat grass, and bees make honey from flowers that grow on the land.

Many plants get food right from the soil they grow in. They soak it up with their roots. Some animals, such as worms, find their food in the soil.

Many animals get their food from the land. These sheep are eating grass.

Sometimes we don't use the land. We just enjoy it.

We look at the Rocky Mountains or the Grand Canyon. We stand in a forest of pine trees or a garden full of roses. Then we know that land is important because it is so beautiful.

Millions of people visit the Grand Canyon every year.

What Can Happen to Land?

It is easy to harm the land. Sometimes people put **poisons** in the soil to kill weeds and insects. Sometimes they put **fertilizers** in the soil to make plants grow bigger. Too many of these things are bad for the soil. After a while, plants won't grow anymore. Sometimes animals die.

Wind can blow soil away. Water can wash it away. This is called **erosion**. Sometimes erosion just happens. But sometimes people make it happen.

These cliffs were formed by soil erosion.

A farmer might leave a whole field bare or put too many cattle in one place and let them eat it bare. Bare soil soon blows or washes away.

Cutting down too many trees can make erosion happen. The roots of trees and plants help hold soil in place.

People also harm the land by dumping trash. Some put their trash in huge, **open dumps**. Open dumps are smelly and ugly. Rats live there and spread diseases.

Some people put their trash in **landfills**. The trash is covered with soil and new trash goes on top. Landfills are cleaner than open dumps. But we are running out of places to put them.

Open trash dumps are not good for people or our land.

Sometimes people put wastes on land. Wastes are left over after burning or making something. Some wastes can harm or even kill living things.

Bad ways of **mining** also harm the land. Some miners just tear the land away and leave big scars behind.

Litter is a problem, too. It looks ugly, and an animal might eat it and get sick.

Many countries set aside land that belongs to everyone. This is called public land. The government takes care of it.

But governments do not always do a good job. They let some people cut down too many trees, mine, dig for oil, or kill animals. This makes all the people poorer, because their land has been harmed.

Too many trees are being cut down. Trees are important to all living things.

These children are planting a new tree.

What Can We Do?

People can stop harming the land. Farmers can stop using poisons and fertilizers that harm the soil. They can use safe **pest** killers and fertilizers.

Soon, special new plants may help them grow better crops. Farmers can keep plants in all their fields. They can give cattle more land to feed on. This would be better for the cattle, too.

Better ways of farming will help stop erosion. But people must also stop cutting down so many trees. They must plant new trees. People must stop dumping so much trash, too. They can **recycle** things. Used cans, glass, paper, and plastic can be made into new things.

People must put harmful wastes in very safe places so they will not hurt people or animals.

People can use better ways of mining. They can stop littering and clean up old litter. They can ask governments to take better care of public land.

People can do many things to care for our land. Some will be hard work. Some will cost money. But we must do them.

What Can You Do?

You can help care for the land, too. Here are some things you can do.

- Talk to your family about recycling, if you don't already do it. Tell them it's important and promise to help.

- Don't litter—ever. Clean up litter when you can.

- Don't ask for junk toys. They will soon break and end up as trash.

- Use things over and over. Take your lunch in a lunchbox, not a paper bag. Take a cloth bag to the store and put the things you buy in it.

- Spend some time just looking at the land around your home. What is beautiful about it? How could people make it more beautiful?

Recycling is one way that you can help save our land.

Words to Know

erosion (e RO zhun)—The wearing away of soil by wind or water.

fertilizer (FUR til eye zer)—A substance used to make plants grow better.

land—The part of the earth that is not covered with water.

landfill—A place where trash is dumped and covered with soil.

litter—Trash put in the wrong place.

mining—Taking rocks and stones that are useful to people out of the ground.

open dump—A place where trash lies on top of the land.

pest—A plant or animal that harms crops.

poison—A thing that is harmful to people, animals, and plants.

recycle—To make something new from something used; to use something again.

root—The part of a tree or plant that is most often under the ground.

Learn More

Books

Orme, Helen. *Pollution.* New York: Bearport Publishing, 2009.

O'Ryan, Ellie. *Easy to Be Green: Simple Activities You Can Do to Save the Earth.* New York: Simon & Schuster, 2009.

Rapp, Valerie. *Protecting Earth's Land.* Minneapolis: Lerner Publishing, 2008.

Threadgould, Tiffany. *ReMake It!: Recycling Projects from the Stuff You Usually Scrap.* New York: Sterling Publishing, 2011.

Web Sites

Kids Recycling Zone.
   <http://kidsrecyclingzone.com>

Save the Earth for Kids.
   <http://savetheearthforkids.com>

Index

A
animals, 5, 6, 7, 14, 18
  cattle, 12, 17
  sheep, 7
  worms, 6

D
dumps, open, 12, 13

E
earth, 5
erosion, 10, 11, 12, 17
  causes of, 10, 12

F
farming, 12, 17
fertilizers, 10, 17

G
Grand Canyon, 8, 9

L
land
  beauty of, 5, 9, 20
  as home for animals, 6
  importance of, 5, 6–9
  as source of food, 6, 7
landfills, 12
litter, 14, 18, 20

M
mining methods, 14, 18

P
people, 6
plants, 6, 10, 17
  roots of, 12
poisons, 10, 17
public land, 14, 18
  care of, 14, 18

R
recycling, 17, 20, 21
Rocky Mountains, 9

S
soil, 4, 5, 6, 10–12
  parts of, 4

T
trash, 12, 13, 17, 19, 20
trees, 12, 14, 15, 16, 17
  roots of, 12

W
wastes, 14, 18
  dangers of, 14
water, 5
  as home for animals, 6